MEAT
RECIPES

Heaven sends us good meat
David Garrick

SALMON

Index

Cover pictures *front: 'A Family Group' by William R. C. Watson   back: 'Mother and Son' by George Rankin title page: 'Wild White Cattle' by Sir Edwin Landseer R.A.*

Printed and Published by J. Salmon Ltd., Sevenoaks, England © Copyright

Steak and Kidney Pudding

*This is one of the oldest and finest of classic British dishes. Serve
direct from the basin, tied round with a fresh, white napkin.*

1½ lb stewing steak	4 oz chopped onions
½ lb ox kidney	1 dessertspoon chopped parsley
1 oz seasoned flour	Salt and pepper

½ - ¾ pint beef stock

PASTRY

2 lb flour   1 oz baking powder   ¼ oz salt   1 lb shredded suet   Cold water to mix

For the pastry, mix all the dry ingredients together in a bowl and mix with
sufficient cold water to produce a stiff, elastic dough which leaves the side of the
bowl cleanly. Roll out on a floured surface and use threequarters to line a greased
2 to 3 pint pudding basin. Cut the beef and kidney into cubes and toss in the
seasoned flour. Fill the lined basin with alternate layers of beef, kidney and
chopped onion, sprinkling each layer with parsley, salt and pepper. When full, put
in any left-over flour, add sufficient stock nearly to cover the meat, put on a pastry
lid, moisten the edges and seal. Cover with greased greaseproof paper and cover
and seal with kitchen foil. Put into a large pan of boiling water, half way up the
basin and steam for 4 hours, topping up the water as necessary. Serve with boiled
potatoes and Brussels sprouts, with a jug of hot water to thin the gravy, if required.
Serves 6 to 8.

Irish Stew

This savoury winter lamb stew is one of the oldest of all Irish recipes. The bones boiled with a carrot and an onion can be used to make the stock.

2 lb neck of lamb, middle or scrag end	**2 tablespoons fresh chopped parsley**
Seasoned flour	**1 teaspoon fresh chopped thyme**
2 large onions, sliced	**Salt and black pepper**
1 lb peeled potatoes, sliced	**$\frac{1}{2}$ -$\frac{3}{4}$ pint water or stock**

Chopped parsley to garnish

Set oven to 325° F or Mark 3. Carefully cut all the meat from the bones with a sharp knife, trim off any excess fat, cut up any of the larger pieces if necessary and coat with seasoned flour. Layer the meat, onions and potatoes in a casserole dish, sprinkling herbs and seasoning between each of the layers and finish with a neat layer of potatoes on top. Pour in sufficient water or stock to come about halfway up the filling, cover the dish with a piece of buttered greaseproof paper and put on the casserole lid. Cook in the oven for 2 to 2½ hours or, alternatively, simmer on top of the stove for about the same time, until the lamb is tender. When ready, skim off any excess fat, spoon the stew into a warmed serving dish with some of the liquid and sprinkle liberally with chopped parsley. Serve the rest of the liquid in a gravy boat. Traditional accompaniments to Irish Stew are boiled carrots and pickled red cabbage. Serves 4.

Pork Cutlets with Turnips

A very simple yet tasty dish. Use small, young turnips for the best flavour.

8 pork cutlets (about 6 oz each)　　　　**1 teaspoon sugar**
2 oz butter　　　　**Salt and pepper**
3 - 4 small turnips, peeled and sliced thickly　**1 - 1½ pints beef or pork stock**

Melt the butter in a pan and brown the cutlets on both sides. Remove and set aside. In the same pan, fry the turnip slices, sprinkling with the sugar to help browning. When brown, replace the cutlets in the pan, season with salt and pepper and add sufficient stock just to cover them. Cover with a lid and simmer gently for about 1 hour until the meat is tender. Transfer the cutlets and turnips to a warm serving dish. Boil hard the remaining liquid in the pan to reduce and thicken and then pour over the meat. Serves 8.

Beef Loaf

An economical supper dish which can be eaten hot or cold. Use best quality minced beef.

1½ lb raw minced beef
3 oz fresh white breadcrumbs
1 onion, finely chopped
1 tablespoon tomato ketchup
Dash of Worcestershire sauce

½ level teaspoon dried mixed herbs
1 teaspoon made English mustard
1 large egg, beaten
¼ pint beef stock
Salt and black pepper

Set oven to 350°F or Mark 4. Grease a 2 lb loaf tin. Mix all the ingredients together thoroughly in a bowl. Put the mixture into the tin and press down firmly. Cook in the oven for 1 hour and cover the top with a piece of greaseproof paper if it appears to be browning too quickly. Turn out and serve either hot, immediately, with potatoes and vegetables or cold with salad. Serves 4 to 6.

Veal Cutlet Pie

This mashed potato covered pie is said to have originated in a Cambridge college and is traditionally served with tomato ketchup.

8 veal loin cutlets (about 6 oz each)	**6 oz chopped celery**
4 oz streaky bacon, chopped	**Salt and black pepper**
1 oz lard	**1¼ pints chicken stock**
8 oz chopped onions	**1½ lb creamed mashed potatoes**
6 oz chopped carrots	**Butter for dotting**

Set oven to 450° F or Mark 8. First cook sufficient potatoes in salted water, mash and cream with a little milk. Melt the lard in a large pan and fry the cutlets gently until light brown. Add the onions, carrots and celery and fry for a few minutes without browning. Season with salt and pepper and add the stock. Cover with a lid and simmer for about 30 minutes. Then, transfer to an ovenproof dish, spread the mashed potatoes over the top, dot with butter and bake in the oven until well browned. Serve with a green vegetable. Serves 8.

Creamed Pheasant Casserole

Birds of an uncertain age or frozen storage are converted into this tender treat.

A brace of pheasants   2 sticks celery, sliced   1 carrot, sliced
1 onion, sliced   1 bay leaf   Salt and black pepper
SAUCE

2 large onions, chopped	**4 tablespoons mango chutney**
Oil for frying	**2 tablespoons Worcestershire sauce**
2 oz flour	**1 tablespoon mushroom ketchup**
220 fl.oz crème fraiche	**1 small tin peaches in juice**

1 tablespoon chopped fresh parsley

Trim the pheasants, put into a large pan with the stock ingredients and cover with water. Bring to the boil then simmer for 1½ to 2 hours until the pheasants are very tender. Leave to cool in the liquid. When cool, strip the meat from the bones and skin, cut into neat pieces and reserve. Strain the stock. Heat the oil in a large pan and fry the onions until soft but not browned. Add the flour, stir in 8 fl. oz of the stock and bring to the boil stirring, to thicken. Remove from the heat and stir in the crème fraiche, chutney and sauces. Stir in the pheasant meat and if the sauce is too thick thin down with a little more stock. Transfer to an ovenproof dish. Drain the peaches very well and cut into cubes. Before serving, stir half the peach cubes into the mixture and reheat for about 20 to 30 minutes until bubbling hot. Garnish with the remaining peaches and chopped parsley and serve. Serves 6 to 8.

Bacon, Cheese and Leek Pie

Use inexpensive bacon pieces to make this tasty family meal. Do not add extra salt without testing as the bacon may be salty enough.

12 oz sliced leeks
12 oz bacon pieces, cut into small dice
Butter and oil for frying
1½ oz flour
12 fl.oz milk

4 oz Lancashire cheese, crumbled
White pepper
Pinch grated nutmeg
1 lb puff pastry
Beaten egg for glazing

Set oven to 425° F or Mark 7. Sauté the leeks in a little butter and oil for 2 to 3 minutes to soften, then set aside. Next, in the saucepan gently fry the bacon cubes to soften but not brown and put with the leeks. Stir the flour into the fat in the pan, adding a little more if necessary and then gradually blend in the milk over a low heat stirring, to thicken. Stir the crumbled cheese into the hot sauce and season with pepper and nutmeg. Return the leeks and bacon to the sauce, stir well together and transfer to a 1½ pint pie dish. Test for seasoning and add salt if necessary. Roll out the pastry on a floured surface, line the edge of the dish with a strip of pastry, dampen and put on a pastry lid. Trim and decorate, make a steam hole and brush with beaten egg. Bake for 15 minutes, reduce oven to 375°F or Mark 5 and bake for about 20 minutes more until the pastry is golden. Serve with mashed potatoes and Brussels sprouts or broccoli. Serves 4.

Pumpkin Pork

Fresh pumpkin with dried apricots give a different flavour to this casserole of pork.

1 lb boneless pork, cubed	2 sticks celery, sliced
2 tablespoons oil	2 oz dried apricots, quartered
1 onion, diced	1 pint vegetable stock
1 clove garlic, chopped	Salt and pepper
12 oz peeled pumpkin, cubed	3 oz fresh breadcrumbs
1 red pepper, chopped	1 clove garlic, crushed
2 carrots, sliced	1 tablespoon oil

1 dessertspoon cornflour

Set oven to 350° F or Mark 4. Heat the oil in a casserole dish and brown the pork cubes on all sides. Set aside and fry the onion and garlic until browned. Replace the pork and add the pumpkin, red pepper, carrots, celery and apricots. Pour over the stock, season and stir together. Bring to the boil, cover and cook in the oven for about 1 hour until the meat is tender. Meanwhile fry the breadcrumbs and crushed garlic in the oil until browned. Dissolve the cornflour in a little water and, when the meat is ready, stir into the casserole, bring to the boil and simmer for a minute or two to thicken. Transfer to a serving dish and keep warm. Just before serving, sprinkle over the browned breadcrumbs. Serves 4 to 6.

Stuffed Breast of Lamb

*This dish, known as Lamb Rosettes, uses inexpensive breast of lamb,
with kidneys and sausage meat.*

2 breasts of lamb, boned
9 oz lamb's kidneys, cored and chopped
12 oz sausage meat
1½ oz butter
Salt and pepper

1 large egg, beaten
2 lbs potatoes, peeled and thinly sliced
6 oz chopped onions
8 oz tomatoes, skinned and thinly sliced
1 tablespoon flour

½ pint beef or lamb stock

Set oven to 350°F or Mark 4. First make the stuffing. Lightly fry the chopped
kidneys and sausage meat in half of the butter and season. Remove from the heat
and bind with the beaten egg. Spread the stuffing over the breasts, roll up and tie
securely with string. Fry the rolls quickly in their own fat to seal, remove from the
pan and cut into 1 inch thick slices. Fry the potatoes, onions and tomatoes in the
fat for a few minutes, adding some or all of the remaining butter, as necessary.
Spread the vegetable mixture over the base of a casserole dish and arrange the lamb
slices on top. Stir the flour into the fat in the pan, add the stock and bring to the
boil to thicken. Pour over the meat, cover and cook in the oven for 2 to 3 hours until
tender. Before serving, skim off surplus surface fat. Serve with boiled or mashed
potatoes and green vegetables. Serves 6 to 8.

Monday Moussaka

Meat and vegetables left over from a Sunday lunch can easily be converted into this tasty and economical dish.

12 oz approx. cooked meat (beef or lamb left over from a Sunday joint)
Cooked, left-over vegetables   ½ pint gravy or beef stock
1 dessertspoon Worcestershire sauce   1 dessertspoon mushroom ketchup
2 tomatoes, sliced   1½ lb potatoes, peeled and sliced
½ pint white sauce   2 oz approx. grated cheddar cheese

Set oven to 350°F or Mark 4. Mince the meat and put into an ovenproof dish. Mix in any left-over vegetables and gravy (or make up some beef stock) and stir in the Worcestershire sauce and mushroom ketchup. Cover with the sliced tomatoes and then with the sliced potatoes. Make up ½ pint white sauce with 1½ oz butter melted with 1½ oz flour, stir in ½ pint of milk and thicken, stirring over a gentle heat. Pour the white sauce over the potatoes and cover with a thick layer of grated cheese. Cook in the oven for about 45 minutes until bubbling and browned on top. Serve with a side salad and crusty French bread. Serves 4.

Stewed Liver and Bacon

This dish makes a change from liver and bacon fried in the usual way and any type of liver can be used.

1 lb liver	**Salt and black pepper**
Seasoned flour	**½ pint beef stock**
½ lb bacon rashers, de-rinded	**½ - ¾ lb potatoes, peeled and sliced**
4 onions, peeled and sliced	**A little melted butter**

Set oven to 350°F or Mark 4. Wipe and trim the liver, then cut into narrow slices and dust with seasoned flour. Fry the bacon lightly, preferably in its own fat. Remove the bacon from the pan and set aside. Add a little cooking oil to the pan, if necessary, and lightly fry the liver and onions. Arrange the liver, onions and bacon in layers in an ovenproof dish, seasoning each layer well. Pour over the stock and top with the sliced potatoes. Cover with a lid or kitchen foil and bake for about ½ hour. Remove the cover, brush the potatoes with melted butter and bake for about 20 minutes more until the liver is cooked and the potatoes are brown. Serves 4 to 6.

'Friends' by Thomas Sidney Cooper R.A.

Mustard Beef Rolls

These appetising rolls of tender topside are filled with mushrooms and wholegrain mustard.

1½ lb topside of beef
6 - 8 teaspoons wholegrain mustard
2 oz button mushrooms, finely chopped
1 oz butter
1 small onion, chopped

2 rashers streaky bacon, chopped
2 tablespoons flour
1 large tin chopped tomatoes
2 tablespoons fresh chopped parsley
Pinch sugar

Salt and black pepper

Set oven to 350°F or Mark 4. Cut the topside into 6 or 8 thin, flat slices. Next, spread each slice with a tablespoon of mustard and sprinkle with chopped mushrooms. Roll up the slices very carefully and secure with cocktail sticks. Place the rolls, side by side, in an ovenproof dish. Melt the butter in a pan and fry the onion and bacon until the onion has softened. Add the flour and cook for another minute. Gradually stir in the tomatoes and simmer gently until the sauce thickens. Remove the sauce from the heat, pass through a sieve and return to the pan. Stir in the parsley and sugar, season and pour over the beef rolls. Put in the oven and cook for about 1 hour, turning the rolls occasionally. Serve with mashed potatoes. Serves 4.

Rabbit Casserole

*A real taste of the countryside. Either joint a whole fresh rabbit
or use prepared joints, if available.*

6 – 8 rabbit joints	1 tablespoon Demerara sugar
Seasoned flour	1 tablespoon French mustard
2 oz butter	1 pint chicken stock
1 large onion, sliced	A bay leaf
2 streaky bacon rashers, diced	Salt and pepper
Chopped fresh parsley to garnish	

Set oven to 300° F or Mark 2. Wash the rabbit joints in cold water, pat dry with kitchen paper and roll in the seasoned flour. Melt the butter in a flameproof casserole and brown the rabbit pieces. Add the onion and bacon and cook for 2 to 3 minutes. Dissolve the sugar and mustard in the stock and pour over the rabbit. Add the bay leaf and season with salt and pepper. Bring slowly to simmering point, cover and cook in the oven for 1½ to 2 hours or until the meat is tender. Sprinkle with chopped parsley before serving with mashed potatoes. Serves 4.

Honeyed Duck Breasts

Plump duck breasts roasted and served with a tasty honey, lemon and port wine sauce.

4 duck breasts	**4 level teaspoons clear honey**
	SAUCE
1 small onion, finely chopped	**2 tablespoons port wine**
¼ pint chicken stock	**1 teaspoon Worcestershire sauce**
Grated rind and juice 1 lemon	**1 teaspoon mushroom ketchup**
1 tablespoon clear honey	**Salt and black pepper**
1 dessertspoon cornflour	**Watercress to garnish**

Set oven to 350°F or Mark 4. Dry the breasts with kitchen paper and fry quickly, skin side down, in a hot pan to brown the skin and melt off some of the fat. Drain and arrange, skin side up, in a roasting tin. Pour a teaspoon of honey over each breast and roast in the oven for about 15 to 20 minutes or until tender. When cooked as preferred, set aside and keep hot. For the sauce, add the onion to the juices in the pan and fry until lightly browned. Stir in the stock, lemon rind and juice and honey. Blend the cornflour with the port wine, stir into the pan with the sauces, season and simmer, stirring, for 2 minutes to thicken. To serve, cut the duck breasts diagonally into thin slices, arrange on warmed plates, pour over a little sauce and garnish with watercress. Serve with creamed potatoes and green peas. Serves 4.

Ham Beresford

A quick and attractive light lunch or supper dish.

8 thin slices cooked ham	**4 hard boiled eggs**
8 plump asparagus spears	**Salt and pepper**
½ oz butter	**¾ pint cheese sauce**

4 tomatoes, skinned and sliced

SAUCE

1½ oz butter	**6 oz Cheddar cheese, grated**
½ oz flour	**1 teaspoon made English mustard**
¾ pint milk	**Salt and pepper**

Set oven to 325°F or Mark 3. Butter an ovenproof dish. Wrap each piece of ham around a trimmed asparagus spear and arrange in the dish. Cut the hard boiled eggs into quarters and set between the ham rolls and season. SAUCE: Melt the butter in a pan, add the flour and cook for 1 minute. Remove from the heat and gradually stir in the milk. Return to the heat and stir constantly until the sauce thickens. Stir in the grated cheese and mustard and season. Pour the sauce over the ham rolls, arrange the tomato slices on top and bake for about 20 minutes until bubbling. Serve with a green salad and wholemeal bread. Serves 4.

Casserole of Lamb Chops

This simple type of pot roast originally used mutton chops and comes from County Durham where it is known locally as Panjotheram.

8 lamb chops	**3 - 4 onions, sliced**
Seasoned flour	**1 pint beef stock,**
1½ - 2 lb potatoes, peeled and sliced	**thickened with a little flour**

Salt and black pepper

Set oven to 325°F or Mark 3. Dry the chops with kitchen paper and dust with seasoned flour. In a casserole dish, arrange layers of potatoes and onions, seasoning each layer well. Bring the stock to the boil and pour sufficient over the vegetables to come half way up them. Arrange the chops on top of the vegetables, cover and cook for 1½ to 2 hours, adding more hot stock, if necessary, during cooking. Serve with boiled carrots and a green vegetable. Serves 4.

Steak and Mustard Pie

A classic English favourite, served with boiled potatoes and green vegetables.

1½ lb rump steak, cubed	½ pint hot water
1½ tablespoons seasoned flour	3 teaspoons prepared English mustard
1 oz butter	Salt and black pepper
1 tablespoon oil	1¼ lb shortcrust pastry
1 large onion, chopped	1 tablespoon chopped fresh parsley
6 oz small button mushrooms, quartered	1egg white

Set oven to 425° F or Mark 7. Grease a 2½ to 3 pint pie dish. Dust the meat with seasoned flour and fry in the butter and oil until browned all over. Remove and set aside. Fry the onion and mushrooms until golden and add to the meat. Pour the hot water into the pan, stir in 2 teaspoons of the mustard and bring to the boil to de-glaze the pan. Season with salt and pepper and set aside. Roll out the pastry on a floured surface and use about two thirds to line the pie dish, up and over the rim. Spoon in the meat, onions and mushrooms, add the mustard stock and sprinkle over the parsley. Damp the pastry rim, cover with a lid and seal and trim. Make a steam hole. Mix the egg white with the remaining teaspoon of mustard and brush over the pastry. Bake for 20 minutes, reduce oven to 350°F or Mark 4 and cook for a further 20 minutes, covering the top with greaseproof paper if it is browning too quickly. Serves 4 to 6.

'On Guard' by Thomas Sidney Cooper R.A.

Pork Chops Savoy

Succulent pork chops cooked in a sweet apple sauce flavoured with Madeira wine or she rry.

4 thick pork chops   1 oz butter
¼ lb cooking apples, peeled, cored and diced
2 oz sultanas   1 teaspoon grated lemon peel
3 fl.oz Madeira wine or sweet sherry   ¼ pint pork stock
1 oz cornflour

Melt the butter in a pan and fry the chops on both sides over a high heat until browned. Remove from the heat and add the apples, sultanas and grated lemon peel. Mix the Madeira or sherry with the stock, pour into the pan and season. Cover and simmer for 1 to 1½ hours; or transfer to a casserole dish, cover and cook in the oven, 350ºF or Mark 4, for a similar time. Transfer the chops to a serving dish and keep warm. Thicken the sauce with cornflour blended with a little water and pour over the chops. Serve with roast potatoes. Serves 4.

Rich Venison Casserole

This casserole has a rich, game taste and is full of flavour.

2 lb venison, cubed	5 fl.oz port wine
2 tablespoons vegetable oil or dripping	8 oz cranberries
4 oz smoked bacon rashers, diced	8 oz chestnuts
1 large onion, roughly diced	4 oz button mushrooms
1 oz flour	1 bay leaf
1½ pints beef stock	Salt and pepper

3 fl.oz double cream

Set oven to 275°F or Mark 1. Heat the fat in a flameproof casserole and brown the venison cubes. Add the bacon and onion and cook for 3 to 4 minutes. Stir in the flour and cook for 1 minute, then pour in the stock and port wine and add the cranberries, chestnuts, mushrooms and bay leaf. Season to taste. Bring slowly to simmering point, cover and cook in the oven for 2 to 2½ hours or until the meat is tender. Remove from the oven and stir in the cream. Serve with creamy mashed potatoes and a green vegetable. Serves 6.

Fricasée of Lamb

The smooth lemon flavoured sauce makes a perfect accompaniment to the meat.

1½ - 2 lb boned shoulder of lamb, cubed

Cooking oil	**Rind and juice 2 lemons**
1½ oz flour	**2-3 sprigs lemon thyme**
4 fl.oz white wine	**Black pepper**
2 cloves garlic, crushed	**2 egg yolks**
1 pint chicken stock	**Chopped fresh parsley to garnish**

Set oven to 325°F or Mark 3. Heat a little oil in a pan and brown the lamb pieces. Transfer to a casserole dish and sprinkle over the flour. Cook for a minute then add the wine and garlic and stir in the chicken stock. Add the lemon peel and thyme, season, bring to the boil, stir and then cover and cook in the oven for about 1½ hours or until the meat is tender. When cooked, discard the lemon peel and thyme and drain off the liquid and reserve. Blend the egg yolks and lemon juice together in a bowl. In a pan, re-heat the reserved liquid, stir a little of it into the egg yolks, mix well and return to the pan. Bring to the boil, whisking and then pour over the meat. Check the seasoning and return the casserole to the oven and cook for about a further 20 minutes. Transfer to a warmed serving dish, garnish with chopped parsley and serve with mashed potatoes. Serves 6.

Pork Parcels

A quick way to serve succulent pork chops in a herby tomato sauce.

4 loin pork chops   6 oz courgettes, thinly sliced
1 medium cooking apple, peeled, cored and chopped
1 large tin chopped tomatoes   1 tablespoon tomato purée
$\frac{1}{2}$ teaspoon sugar   1 teaspoon dried sage
Salt and black pepper

Set oven to 350°F or Mark 4. Place each chop on a piece of kitchen foil large enough to wrap it completely. Put all the other ingredients into a bowl and mix together. Spoon one quarter of the mixture on to each chop and wrap up the foil securely to make a loose parcel. Put the parcels in a roasting tin and cook for about 50 to 55 minutes. When cooked, unwrap carefully, put the chops on warmed plates and pour over any liquid in the foil. Serve with potatoes and a green vegetable. Serves 4.

Sausage Cobbler

Use plump butcher's sausages, either plain or herby flavoured, as personal choice.

**1 lb sausages   Oil for frying   2 onions, sliced   4 oz streaky bacon, diced
1 oz flour   1 large tin chopped tomatoes   2 tablespoons tomato purée
1 tablespoon Worcestershire sauce   1 tablespoon mushroom ketchup
½ pint beef stock   Salt and black pepper   3 oz button mushrooms, halved**

SCONE TOPPING

8 oz self-raising flour	**1 teaspoon dry mustard powder**
Pinch of salt	**2 oz butter, softened**
1 teaspoon baking powder	**1 egg, beaten ¼ pint milk**

Set oven to 425°F or Mark 7. First cut the sausages into 2 or 3 sections and fry gently in a large pan until browned. Transfer to a dish and keep warm. Fry the onions and bacon until soft, then add the flour and fry for a minute longer. Add the tomatoes, tomato purée, sauces and stock, season and bring to the boil, stirring. Add the mushrooms and sausage pieces, simmer for 15 to 20 minutes, then transfer to an ovenproof dish. Meanwhile, make the scone topping. Sift the flour, salt, baking powder and mustard into a bowl and rub in the butter. Add the egg and stir in sufficient milk to mix to a soft dough. Roll out to ½ inch thickness on a floured surface, cut out into small scones with a cutter and arrange, overlapping, around the edge of the sausage mixture in the dish. Bake in the oven for about 15 minutes until the scones are risen and golden brown. Serves 4.

Chicken and Leek Pie

Before serving, this pie is enriched with double cream, making it a simplified modern version of a medieval recipe.

2 lb raw diced chicken	Pinch ground nutmeg
Oil for frying	Pinch ground mace
8 slices ham, diced	½ pint chicken stock
1 medium leek, sliced	Salt and pepper
2 medium onions, chopped	¾ lb shortcrust pastry
1 tablespoon sugar	Beaten egg to glaze

½ pint double cream

Set oven to 350° or Mark 4. Grease a 3 pint pie dish. Lightly fry the chicken pieces in a little oil, without browning. Layer the dish with ham, leeks, onion, chicken, onion and leeks, finishing with ham on top. Pour in sufficient stock nearly to cover and season with the spices and salt and pepper. Roll out the pastry on a floured surface, use to cover the pie and trim. Make a steam hole. Brush with beaten egg and bake for 1 hour until the chicken is cooked and the pastry is golden brown. If the pastry browns too quickly, cover with a piece of greaseproof paper. When cooked, heat the double cream (do not boil), open out the steam hole, pour the hot cream into the pie (a funnel is useful) and serve. Serves 8.

'The Foster Mother' by Frank Paton

Bacon Olives

These bacon rolls are stuffed with any left-over cooked meat, chicken, turkey, pork or ham for example, and can be used as a quick snack or to form the basis for a more satisfying meal.

8 large rashers smoked back bacon	1 dessertspoon chopped fresh parsley
4 oz cooked meat, minced	Salt and pepper
2 oz breadcrumbs	Pinch of mixed herbs
1 tablespoon finely chopped onion	1 egg, beaten

Set oven to 350° F or Mark 4. In a bowl, mix together the minced meat with the breadcrumbs, onion and parsley, season with salt and pepper and a pinch of mixed herbs and bind with the beaten egg. Spread a layer of the mixture over each of the bacon rashers, roll up carefully and tie with thin string or spear with cocktail sticks. Place the olives in a greased baking tin and bake for about 15 minutes until heated through and the bacon is cooked. Serve on their own for a quick snack or with fried eggs and sauté potatoes for a light meal. Serves 4.

Devilled Lamb Cutlets

Devilling refers to any spicy mixture, not necessarily curry, which is used to flavour meat.

8 lamb cutlets (about 6 oz each)	**1 tablespoon mushroom ketchup**
½ lb butter, softened	**1½ oz dry mustard powder**
1 tablespoon Worcestershire sauce	**Salt and white pepper**
	Cayenne pepper

Trim the cutlets, put under a hot grill and cook for about 10 to 15 minutes, turning once. Transfer to a serving dish and keep warm. Meanwhile, in a bowl, mix together the butter, Worcestershire sauce and mushroom ketchup and season very well with salt, white pepper and a good amount of cayenne pepper, to taste. Spread the devil mixture over the cutlets just before serving. Serve with potatoes and green vegetables or on a bed of rice. Serves 8.

Peppered Steaks

*The meat is fried encrusted with crushed peppercorns and served
with a brandy flavoured cream sauce.*

4 sirloin, rump or fillet steaks
2 tablespoons black peppercorns, crushed
1 oz butter   1 tablespoon oil   Salt
2 tablespoons brandy   ¼ pint double cream

Trim any excess fat from the steaks. Crush the peppercorns, fairly coarsely with a
rolling pin and sprinkle over the steaks. Press down firmly with the fingers, turn
over and repeat on the reverse, to encrust both sides. Heat the butter and oil in a
pan and quickly fry the steaks on both sides to seal. Lower the heat and continue
frying until the meat is cooked to taste. Season with salt. When cooked, carefully
remove from the pan and keep warm. Add the brandy to the hot pan, remove from
the heat and set it alight. When the flames have died away, stir in the cream and
reheat gently (do not boil). Put the steaks on warmed plates, pour over the sauce
and serve immediately with beans or peas and new potatoes. Serves 4.

Lamb Pie

*A very simple meat and vegetable pie which is lifted with the sharp flavour
of gooseberries; a good use for this seasonal fruit.*

1 lb fillet of lamb, diced	**4 oz spinach or cos lettuce**
Salt and pepper	**6 oz gooseberries**
Grated nutmeg	**5 tablespoons chicken or vegetable stock**
Blade of mace	**8 oz shortcrust pastry**

Set oven to 375° F or Mark 5. Grease an 8 inch (approx.) pie dish. Cut the meat
into small pieces and arrange them in the dish. Season with salt, pepper and
nutmeg. Lay the blade of mace on top of the meat. Blanch the spinach (or lettuce)
in boiling water for 1 minute, then drain and lay it on top of the meat. Finally make
a layer of gooseberries. Pour over the stock. Roll out the pastry on a floured
surface, use to cover the pie with a pastry lid and make a steam hole in the centre.
Bake for 1 hour, then cover the pastry with greaseproof paper. Reduce the
temperature to 325°F or Mark 3 and bake for a further 1¾ hours. Serves 4.

Spicy Cottage Pie

*A sweet and spicy variant on a well known theme, with an
egg topping instead of mashed potatoes.*

2 lb lean minced beef
Butter and oil for frying
1 large onion, finely chopped
1 apple, peeled, cored and chopped
1 tablespoon curry powder

1 oz fresh white breadcrumbs
1½ oz flaked almonds
3 oz sultanas
Juice and grated rind 1 lemon
1 egg, beaten

Salt and black pepper
TOPPING
2 eggs   ½ pint milk

Set oven to 350°F or Mark 4. Grease an ovenproof dish. First fry the meat in a little butter and oil until cooked through and set aside. Next, fry the onion and apple with the curry powder for about 5 minutes. Mix the onion mixture with the mince and the breadcrumbs, stir in the almonds, sultanas and lemon juice and rind and the beaten egg and season very well. Transfer to the dish and press down firmly. Make the topping by mixing together the eggs and milk, season and pour over the meat mixture in the dish. Bake for about 1 hour until the topping is bubbling and golden brown. Serve with carrots and green vegetables. Serves 6.

Roast Pork Tenderloin

Meaty tenderloin roasted with a garlic, parsley and lemon filling.
Simple, but ideal for a special occasion.

2 pork tenderloin (about 12 oz each)
Grated rind and juice 2 lemons
6 tablespoons chopped fresh parsley
12 garlic cloves, blanched

Salt and pepper
2-3 bay leaves
2 tablespoons oil
Lemon slices to garnish

Blanch the garlic cloves for a few minutes in boiling water. Split the pork lengthways with a sharp knife without cutting right through. Open each piece out and fold flat. Sprinkle over the grated lemon rind and the parsley. Lay the blanched garlic cloves (halving if too big) along the middle of each fillet and season with salt and pepper. Close up the fillets and tie at 1 inch intervals with string. Put into a porcelain dish with the bay leaves, pour over the lemon juice, cover and leave to marinate overnight in the refrigerator. Next day, set oven to 400°F or Mark 6. Remove the port fillets from the dish and reserve the marinade. Heat the oil in a pan and brown the meat all over. Transfer the meat to a roasting tin with the oil and the marinade, season and roast for about 35 minutes, basting frequently. When cooked, cut into one inch thick slices and serve with lemon slices and sautéed onion rings. Serves 6.

'The Intruders' by Walter Hu

Beef in Guinness

Rich, dark Guinness and caramelised onions give a deep flavour to the gently casseroled meat.

2 lb chuck steak, cubed	1-2 cloves garlic, crushed
2 oz seasoned flour	1 teaspoon brown sugar
Oil and butter for frying	1 pint Guinness
2 large onions, sliced	Juice and zest 1 orange

2-3 bay leaves

Set oven to 350° F or Mark 4. Coat the meat in seasoned flour and fry in a little butter and oil until browned all over. Transfer to a casserole dish with any remaining flour. Next, gently fry the onions and garlic until softened then add the sugar, increase to a moderate heat and cook for a further minute to caramelise the sugar. Put into the casserole with the meat, pour over the Guinness, add the orange juice and bay leaves and bring to the boil. Cover and cook in the oven for 1½ to 2 hours until the meat is tender. If the gravy becomes too thick, add a little more water. When ready, discard the bay leaves, sprinkle over the orange zest and serve with mashed potatoes and green vegetables. Serves 4 to 6.

Kidneys in Onions

Choose large, well formed onions for this dish, which can be eaten as an entrée
or for a light lunch or supper; one onion and kidney for each person.

8 large onions (about 6 oz each)   **¾ - 1 pint beef stock**
8 lamb's kidneys   **5 fl.oz red wine**
1 tablespoon cornflour

Set oven to 350°F or Mark 4. Peel the onions, slightly trim the bases so that they stand upright and cut off the top portion to form lids. Carefully scoop out the centre of each onion so that a kidney will just fit into the hollow. Trim the kidneys, put each one into an onion and replace the lid. Put the onions into a casserole dish and pour in sufficient stock to come halfway up the onions. Cover and cook in the oven for 1 hour. Then add the red wine and cook for a further 30 minutes. Transfer the onions to individual warmed bowls and keep warm. Boil the liquid hard to reduce slightly, thicken with blended cornflour and pour over the onions to serve. Serve with crusty bread. Serves 8.